PANIC ATTACKS
and ME

PANIC ATTACKS and ME

KAY HAMMOND

Copyright © 2020 Kay Hammond.

All rights reserved. No part of this book may be reproduced in any form or by any electronic or mechanical means, including information storage and retrieval systems, without permission in writing from the publisher, except by reviewers, who may quote brief passages in a review.

ISBN: 978-1-63684-592-0 (Paperback Edition)
ISBN: 978-1-63684-593-7 (Hardcover Edition)
ISBN: 978-1-63684-591-3 (E-book Edition)

Book Ordering Information

Phone Number: 315 288-7939 ext. 1000 or 347-901-4920
Email: info@globalsummithouse.com
Global Summit House
www.globalsummithouse.com

Printed in the United States of America

Contents

Preface ix
Chapter 1:   Panic Attacks 1
Chapter 2:   Learning Disability 5
Chapter 3:   Money Stresses 9
Chapter 4:   Losing Support by a Move 13
Chapter 5:   Surviving a Disaster 17
Chapter 6:   When People Split... 21
Chapter 7:   Needing Surgery 25
Chapter 8:   Keeping Your Health 29
Chapter 9:   Car Care 31
Chapter 10: Giving to Others 35
Chapter 11: Finding My Way 39
Chapter 12: Emergencies 43
Chapter 13: Trips 45
Chapter 14: Losing Things 49
Chapter 15: Organization 53
Chapter 16: Losing a Pet 57
Poems..61
    Claustrophobic.. 63
    Found 64
    Stress.. 65
    Plan For Me 66
    Dreams 67
    Expectations Met 68
    God Poem... 70

For Mom

PREFACE

Panic attacks have affected more of us than we realize. I had not realized that was what I was experiencing until I had this story critiqued. I had what I now realize felt like panic attacks. I would crawl up on the den sofa as a child and not be able to move, as my mother would yell at me constantly. It seemed as if I could never do anything right. I could not understand what was expected of me.

I am grateful that there were other neighbors who were not as critical of me as my mother. Eventually I would crawl off the sofa and escape to friendlier places. I have said for a long time that the lady across the street was more of a mother to me then my mother. She always had a kind ear to listen to my problems and make me feel better about myself.

My Dad was also my protector from mother. He had to pick his battles for me with her, as there were many. He was more of a teacher than she was. I could never understand what she was trying to teach me if she would even try. She was a stay-at-home mother, so she tried to come between me and Dad, by telling me he was too tired to help me. But I found out that he was always happy to help me. I am sure that it hurt their marriage trying to deal with me. I was told they had to walk on eggshells when really it was the other way around.

The problem was that I have a learning disability. And this was before learning disabilities were understood and there was help for them. While I was growing- up, I was accused of having a "sin over my head". I was always told that. When I was divorced in 1990, I wanted to find out what my sin was, so I got an IQ test. I have an auditory processing problem which means that I have trouble understanding what people are saying at times, especially when they are yelling or being critical which is what my mom would do.

This book is some of the ways that I learned to cope with life and not get paralyzed every time I had a problem. This coping can be transferred to all kinds of losses and panic situations. It taught me how to find the missing things and to find my way. I hope that it will help you also. Panic comes in different situations. It is all solvable if you slow down and put one foot in front of the other.

I have always believed that there was a way to keep out of being paralysis, something that would make sense. As I started getting the idea for this book, I used a recorder when I had ideas for sections of the book. As I would record in various places, people would show great interest.

I have had some form of written transcript for many years. I was wondering what to do with it. Then a creative friend taught me to make chapbooks. That felt really good to have a way to publish it. The chapbooks really sold really well and I also enjoyed giving it to the special people in my life.

I have always wanted more for these words. I am so happy to have discovered this way to get my words out to more people in a better format.

CHAPTER

1

PANIC ATTACKS

According to the National Institute of Mental Health, "panic attacks are a type of anxiety disorder in which you have repeated attacks of intense fear that something bad will occur when unexpected. It most often peaks with in 10 to 20 minutes. Although the symptoms may last longer".

According to Wikipedia, the online encyclopedia, "Panic attacks are periods of intense fear or apprehension that are of sudden onset and relatively brief duration. Often, those afflicted with experience significant- anticipatory anxiety and limited symptoms attacks in between attacks, in situations where attacks have previously occurred."

For me, I do not want to feel like I will loose my life, when I suffer a panic attack. I do not know what to do. How can I find comfort from the pain? Do I need to go to the Emergency Room? Can a doctor help with this problem? Can I just calm down? Will all be ok?

I have to remember that God is in charge. Sometimes you may need to look for a doctor who you can trust to help or who can lead you to one who can. Sometimes doctors can give you the answer that you need and sometimes they can't. But most of the time they can point us to the next right step. All God asks is for us to do the footwork.

Please tell me what needs to be done for me. Not all pains are serious or need medical help. They can be helped by exercise and a proper diet. Find out what is right for you.

When I have panic attacks, how can I get help? How bad are my attacks? I need to know what is normal and what can be a problem. Who do I trust? When I can get the focus away from the fear and count my blessings and be grateful for the things that I do have. One of my causes is financial, but I have lots to be grateful for. When I can turn my finances over to God then I can relax, then these problems will be solved. It takes away the fear with God in charge. We know that fear is one of the main reasons for panic attacks. Turn it over to your Higher Power so you can stay away from the fear.

Take your vitamins and any other necessary pills on a regular basis to stay healthy. Take care of yourself, eat healthy, exercise, and trust in a power greater than you.

We need a Higher Power who can be of help? God can help all of us.

We need to ask God to help. We can choose our Higher Power. It does not need to be the God of our upbringing. The God of my upbringing was shameful and vindictive. I was grateful when I found a loving God!

When I got into Recovery 22 years ago, in 1990, I had a shameful, vindictive God. I was told that I had to find a God who I was comfortable with trusting with my life. I was grateful that others were doing the same process. We talked about all kind of God figures: a feminine figure, the group, nature, the door knob.

The process was rewarding and we were not judged by the figure that would help us.

If we still struggled, we were told that we could lean on some one else's God until we could find one of our own. My God figure has changed over the years. My current church believes that God is every where and in every thing. That works for me now.

CHAPTER

2

LEARNING DISABILITY

I always have had troubles learning. I have trouble with a learning disability called an auditory processing problem. That is according to Wikipedia – the online free encyclopedia, "people with this disorder cannot process the information they hear in the same way as others do, which leads to difficulties in recognizing and interpreting sounds, especially the sounds composing speech."

Do you have trouble learning? Do you need a test to see what your problem is? You might. That is how my disability got discovered. I had an IQ test. I was able to get the test by a wonderful lady with the school system in Houston.

I grew up before learning disabilities were understood. This caused me trouble though out my life. I had lots of trouble learning to read. I had trouble understanding what some people say. My brain does not think fast. Often people were not patient with me. For example, I know that my mother was not patient with me. I felt hopeless and alone. Where could I go for help? It was important to find someone who I could trust to help me. For me, growing up, I would escape to friendly neighbors.

After my diagnosis was discovered in 1990 and after my divorce, my parents thought that the Texas Rehabilitation Commission could help. They are a government agency, in Texas, which helps people to get where they can succeed in the job market.

Learning disabilities are being diagnosis earlier now for the most part. It took me 8 years to find a way to get help through the Texas Rehabilitation Commission. It was well worth it. I had to take Defensive Driving for a speeding ticket. The teacher had a book of business cards. I found a speech therapist in the book and called her. She said that she knew someone who could help me.

It is always in God's time and way not ours. It does not have to be the end of the world. I am very grateful for the woman who said that she could help me and was able to convince the Texas Rehabilitation Commission to pay for the therapy. I also told the Rehab that this lady could help me and to please pay for it as I could not afford to pay for it and I really needed the help. She gave me help to deal with my disability.

Points to remember:

* Stay in the present.
* Look for your choices.
* Write them down.
* Who do you trust?
* Where can you find them?
* Will telling someone help?

I am grateful for the help. It was well worth the wait. I have felt better since the therapy, and I am better able to cope with life and I know that you can feel better too.

God, or the power you trust with your life, will lead you if you ask. Remember it is in God's time not yours. There will be help available if you trust and believe. You can check the Internet. You can check the library for books on the topic. Ask your counselor.

Growing up I was never given choices, so now I really value my choices. I hope that you can have choices also. We always need choices and we frequently need more than one choice. Look for all of your choices. The first choice may not really be the best!

Turn it over to your God! We need a Higher Power who can be of help. God will help all of us. We need to ask our Higher Power to help. We must realize it is in God's time not our, as difficult as that may be to understand. We deserve to feel good about ourselves. At times we may have to practice patience. I was not taught patience, so that has been difficult to learn. But I am trying.

CHAPTER 3

MONEY STRESSES

Having money problems, I could not figure out what to do about it. So I ended up loosing my home. I could not pay the mortgage payment and the loan company ended up taking the house back. Like so many people, I did not know how I can get through it. I know it is happening to lots of people now. But it was different because it is me!

For me, I lost my job, so I lived on credit for a year. I didn't know what was going on. Will I be able to get another job where I live? Or do I need to move in with a friend? Do I need to move into a cheaper place? Do I need to move at all? Moving is usually so expensive. I need to decide if it is necessary. Is there anything that I can do to help? Will I have to let go of things important to me? Or can I put them is storage somewhere? I know I need to figure out what is most important to me. How will I choose?

Points to remember:

* Stay in the present.
* Look for your choices.
* Write down your choices.
* Who do you trust?
* Where can you find them?
* Will telling someone help?
* You need more than one choice.
* The first choice may not really be the best!

When I finally got a steady income, I wanted to pay off my debt. I chose a credit counseling service, because they could cut the amount that I needed to repay. Some of the interest fees they were able to get reduced to nothing, and some of them the percent of interest fees were reduced. They also put me on a repayment schedule. It took 5 years to repay my debt, but it saved my credit and gave me a good feeling of being responsible. The payments were a struggle for the 5 years. I learned to get help from food pantries and other places that help the poor.

I turned it over to God, my guiding force! I needed a Higher Power who could help? God will help all of us. We need to ask God to help.

My Home

CHAPTER

4

LOSING SUPPORT BY A MOVE

To progress in my career, my company is moving me to a new city. Do I want to go? There are choices. Sometime the benefits in moving are greater than staying in the old city. I ended up liking the new city, but did not know much about it. The new job sounded good with a good pay raise. So I decided to move

Things to remember:

- What do you want to learn about your new community?
- What are your interests?
- Is there a tour of your new city? I have enjoyed the tours of the cities that I have gone to visit.
- At your hotel, is there the usual rack of local attractions? I have seen these in many different hotels in many different cities. The yellow pages can be your guide to getting your needs met in the new city. Then you can call the new place for directions. If you go to church, look in the phone book

for available churches similar to the one that you enjoy. A new church home does not have to be made over night. The directory is just a starting point to help get you started.

Are there other things of interest to you and your family? I like to be around water, so that was one of the things what I looked for when I moved here. The new people whom I met were able to tell me of the wonderful water places here. They were fun to explore.

As I was moving here, I had a friend who was moving from here as I came. She was able to help in getting my needs met, like a place to get my haircut. She also gave me other pointers. I really struggled to get my needs met when I moved here. A real frustrating thing was the streets changed names. The lack of street signs also frustrated me. A map of my new town was really valuable and so was my GPS.

I had a dog to walk. That helped me to get to know my neighbors. I have always felt safer knowing my neighbors. I enjoyed taking my dog for outings like to play at the lakes and other parks around. I always felt more comfortable when I had my dog by my side for my security.

When I got homesick for my old home, I had friends to call back there. I was able to share my new life with them. I have always been able to go back for visits.

When I went back to work, that put more structure in my life which gave me more to do and an income. The family that I worked for included me in their lives. But that has not always been true, but it helped me to get settled, as she was able to help me find places to go to get my needs met.

Things to remember:

* What do I enjoy doing?
* Where can I find friends?
* Will there be friends with similar interests?
* Will there be people to do things with?
* Look everywhere you go.
* Trust that your God is in control!

As I learned to get around in my new city, I felt comfortable and was able to get my needs met. I met new friends, both at my new home and at my recovery meetings. My job gave me new friends also.

CHAPTER

5

SURVIVING A DISASTER

Disasters and life lessons happen. So after a fire or a disaster, you are stunned, but need to calm down to see where you need to go from there. Writing about what you are thinking always helps me. When I put it on paper, I can clear my mind of the troubling thoughts. If I feel the need to revisit the painful thought, I have it written down. Then all that I have to do is reread what I have written. Frequently writing it down takes some of the pain out of the experiences and relieves some of the chatter in the mind, so it can be cleared for more important things. There may be things to add as time passes.

Things can be replaced, but what about those special things that can not be replaced? If we have decided what is most important to us, we will be able to get them and not loose even them. What is most important to you?

I need to ask myself: What are the most valuable things to me? What are the things that can not be replaced? One thing for me is my Mother's family bible. Another thing is my camera cards, the negatives of my life in pictures.

How bad was it? Did anyone lose their life? Is anything left of value to me or of value for the family as a whole? Were all things lost? It helps to have something to remember the loss.

Will we be able to rebuild? Do we want to rebuild? Or will we need to start over in a new location? There are choices to be made.

Is there a place to stay for the time being? There may be relatives or friends who give us a place to stay. Sometimes a hotel or motel is simpler than trying to stay with friends, for the short term. Do we need to rent an apartment for the long term?

Maybe pictures will help. Or maybe the memories will be enough. It is important to look for things to be grateful for, as they can help ease the pain.

Points to remember:

* Stay in the present.
* Look for your choices.
* Write down your choices.
* Who do you trust?
* Where can you find them?
* Will telling someone help?

Fire extinguishers are important for home fires, especially if we are aware when they start. Every home should have one under the kitchen sink. Cooking fires are easy to start, but also easy to put out.

Fires need three things to burn: Air, material to burn, and be ignited, or combustion. If we take away the air, by covering the fire, it will go out. Also it needs something to burn.

If a person catches on fire: we were taught in school to stop, drop, and roll. I was taught to stop, lay on the ground and roll.

Burn Out Home

CHAPTER 6

WHEN PEOPLE SPLIT

Being human, some times we have disagreement with people in our lives. Or they chose a different path for their lives. It may not have been anything that we did. It is just God putting us on a different path. If we can chose to see it that way, it might cut down the sting.

What will happen when those we love split, how does this affect us? Where will I go? Will I have any choices? Will my choices be listened to? Whom do I trust? Will this person help me to live where I feel I need to live? Where I want to go or where do I need to go to be safe?

Will I be able to get my needs met? What do I need? I need to list my needs and wants that are important to me, so I can share them with the important people. Whom do I love? Will I be able to keep things important to me?

I suffered a divorce after 13 years of marriage. The abuse escalated and I had had all that I would take. Choices had to be made who got everything. I was given our dog because I was her main caregiver. My ex had spoiled her so terribly, so I could not handle her. So I gave her back to him. He lost her. And because she needed meds, she probably didn't last long. That really hurt! I need to remember: No one lives forever.

My divorce was simple by most standards. All we had to separate was debt, as my ex was a spend thrift. We lived in an apartment. The saddest thing was the dog. I loved her immensely and was sad that she was so spoiled that I could not handle her.

The day that I moved out, I felt like I had been release from hell. Arranging the move was surprisingly easy. All the people that I needed to deal with were really nice and went out of their way to be helpful.

Some people or animals are in our life for a reason and/or a season to teach us something or to give us the love and support that we need at that time. I was really grateful for my recovery friends and their support. At my job, the people there understood of my pain and gave me sympathy and understanding.

Points to remember:

* What are my choices?
* Write them down.
* Where is my support?
* Stay in the present.
* Do you have all that you need?
* Where can you find them?

Look for your choices. We all need choices. Will I continue to have family I can count on? After my divorce only one of my ex's children would be my friend and she lives a long way away. My ex had 6 children and two grandkids. He also had 4 siblings. We never had kids of our own. I went from a large family to a small family. My only sibling is one brother, who has a wife and two kids. At that time, both my parents were alive, but Dad has since died. That hurt, but now I see that there was a reason for it. My biological family may not be the people that I am closest to, and that is ok.

The pastor at my church saw that I needed to have a pet to love. He went with me and pay for my new dog. I was able to find a cute poodle mix. He encouraged me to give her a French name. I called her Bon Chance, which is French for good luck. She was truly my good luck charm. I was also able to get the things that the dog from my marriage had, which as a real blessing, as I did not have much money. We went many places together. I always felt safe when I was with her.

Divorce and/or separation are usually painful. Look for your support. Ask God to help you find some friends. Do you have friends in recovery, thru your church, or thru your job? There are all kinds of places to make friends. These can give you people to share with to lesson the grief. As we talk about our lives the pain will lesson.

CHAPTER

7

NEEDING SURGERY

My body needed help. It is part of being human for our bodies to need help ever so often. Who do I trust to make me well again? Do I know someone who can lead me to where I need to go? Where is someone that I trust? Do I trust that person to lead me to the correct specialist?

When I moved here, I went to a clinic with all kinds of doctors. As I grew to know the doctors in the clinic, I became more comfortable. I have been going to the same family doctor for about 20 years. I trust him to refer me to get my needs met. I have been very grateful for his support and guidance. All that security did not come over night, as I was happy with the doctors who he sent me to.

When I had to have my knee replaced, I was grateful for the friends that I had. I was having trouble accepting what I was experiencing. There was an in-hospital rehab that I was able to go to until I could get around by myself. The most wonderful thing I took with me was a CD player. I forgot extra batteries, but the rehab had some. They had told me what I needed to take, which included clothes to wear. That surprised me. I took some shorts and was glad that I did, as I needed to dress in the in-patient rehab every day.

I was ashamed of feeling the way that I was treating people once I got home. I was ashamed of being dependent on others for my every need. The hurting got the best of me at times. I sure did not want to get hooked on the pain pills. I was able to find a guy in AA who had undergone a knee replacement a month before me. He gave me some idea as to how I should take the pain pills. I was grateful for that help.

Higher Power, I am so grateful for all your handiwork – your love and acceptance. Thank you for putting the people that I needed in to my life at the times that I needed them. One major lesson that I learned was that I could not expect my friends to drop what they were doing to meet my needs immediately. They were happy to do them, but they needed some notice. God, I was tired of asking for help as I expect that my friends were tired of me asking for help. My feelings were that I needed to get over needing help.

I was use to being a giver and not a taker of support. This had been hard for me to keep asking for help. There was a friend who offered to give me a bath. I had to hide me modesty. I was very grateful for people who were able to clean my apartment and other necessary things. I hated to be needy. I have worked so hard to be independent. It hurt to show the needy side of me, even for a little while. I realized that this too shall pass as I got stronger every day.

I missed my alone time. I was able to arrange for many people to help me. I hated to have alternative motives for people to be here. It was hard not to have control of my surroundings, as I could not do for myself all that needed to be done for me. I could not hide the key outside. So I had to leave my door unlocked. This took away some of my security. It helped to realize that this is only temporary as I got better each day.

One thing for sure I have been truly overwhelmed by the love and support that I have experienced. Being open to receiving love has been truly hard for me.

Points to remember:

* Make a list of needs.
* Make a list of what can do for self.
* Make a list of people who will help.
* People need some notice, as they will not drop everything and come.
* Notice the improvements every day as the days pass.

God, help me to accept.
God, help me to be loving.
God, help me to trust.

The help that I got, I will forever be grateful for. My church has an Inreach Ministry. Some of the help that I got came from them, I have been giving back to other people in need. That has really felt good to give back to this special ministry.

CHAPTER

8

KEEPING YOUR HEALTH

These days there is much in the news about eating healthy and exercising regularly. The town that I live in is very health conscious. I am conscious of this and I am aware of exercise and eating healthy. It is also important to take the pills that your doctor has given you for maintenance. It is important to stay away from street drugs and alcohol. They both can kill you. I have known many people to die of both of those.

I do not want to loose my health. So I must take care of myself. If I do not take care of myself, no one else will. Do I know how to eat things that are good for me? Sometimes I can be happy with good foods. It's just often I do not follow it. Am I eating healthy? Do I know what my body needs to be healthy? Do I know how to read labels? What should I look for on labels? Calories are important. I remember what I should be eating fruits, vegetables, and protein.

Not all bad things are high in calories. We need a balance. If we deprive ourselves of all that tastes good, that is not good. We need to find our own balance. If there are only too much of the good things, we cannot stay content.

Diets never work in the long run. As certain as we are to lose the weight on a diet, we are as certain to gain it back. Our way of eating has to be modified.

Points to remember:

* Stay in the present.
* Look for your choices.
* Write down your choices.
* Find someone you trust.
* Where can you find them?
* Will telling someone help?
* You need more than one choice.
* The first choice may not really be the best!
* Turn it over to God or your Higher Power!

Being a lifetime Weight Watcher since the 1970's, I can use their way to eating health. I am grateful for my choices in eating . Sometimes I am better at watching what I eat than others. It seems hard to watch it every day. Some people are better at it than others.

There is more to staying healthy than just eating healthy. There are such things as not smoking or drinking. Brushing your teeth, bathing regularly, and exercising are important. I try to walk daily and ride the exercise bike. Water is good source of fluids. It has been said to drink 8 glasses of water a day. Some days I can do it and some days I can't. I feel better when I do.

A couple of things make life more pleasant: smiling and laughter. I am still working on them. Hugs make me feel good also. I have learned that I can hug myself. That is fun. In my recovery meetings, I get hugs after the meeting. I look forward to them. I have learned to ask before thrush myself on someone.

CHAPTER 9

CAR CARE

Owning a car is a big responsibility that does not end with having a driver's license and a car. Most cars, in Texas, have two stickers on their windshield. One is that the car is registered to drive in the state. The other one is that the car is safe to be on the road. How important are they? If the car is on the road, a ticket can be given with out-of-date stickers. I know. I once got a ticket for my sticker being out of date.

I tried to get my sticker updated. In my state, it was hard to tell which sticker was due. I took my car to the mechanic to be checked for the safety sticker. My insurance certificate had been expired for a couple of days. He would not inspect the car. I needed to go get a current proof of insurance.

Points to remember:

* Where is the information available?
* Stay in the present.
* Look for your choices.

* Write them down.
* Who do you trust?
* Where can you find them?
* Will telling someone help?

I needed more than one choice. The first choice may not really be the best. Turn it over to God! Ask all that can help. Turn it over. If it is meant to be mine, I will find it in God's time. My time is not necessarily God's time. Well, if I can't find it, do I have to have it now? What am I going to do? Do I need it? Is it necessary?

It ended up that I needed to go to one of my insurance company's offices and they gave me a current registration, so I could get my car inspected. My current insurance was not expired. I just did not have the new paper. The car got inspected and all is well. That was the correct sticker that needed to be updated.

Gratitude was with me that day as I was able to get done what needed to be done to have my car safe to be on the road. Do you know what is required of you to have the car safe to be on the road in your state? I understand that different states have different requirements. I am grateful for the requirements in Texas which is less complicated than some states.

It is also necessary to get you oil changed every 3 months to 3000 miles. This keeps the engine running smooth. Another thing to watch out for is the tires. If there is no tread left, the tires will not have traction on the road. No telling where your car will end up, if it does not stay where you intend for it to be.

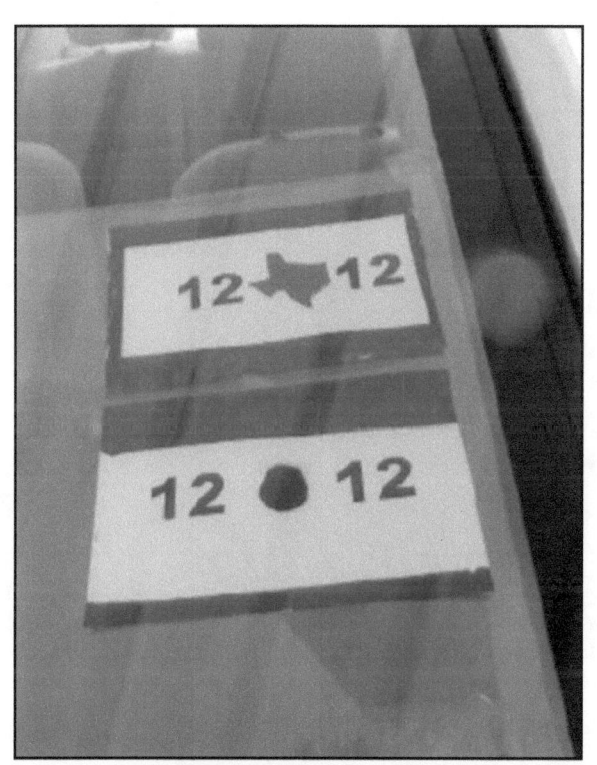
Current Stickers on My Car

CHAPTER

10

GIVING TO OTHERS

Sometimes, people can not afford to have all the things that they need. They have to make choices as to what they can afford. Here in Austin, there are several drives to help people who can not afford to have coats and other necessary things.

When I was in high school, I came home from school without my coat. So of course, Mother asked where it was. I replied it was in my locker. Mother expressed concern. She said that coats are important and need to be taken care of, as coats do not grow on trees.

Then the second day, still there was no coat. I told my Mother that I was not sure where it was. This is where the yelling kicked in. Most coats are expensive. This is where the threats started kicking in, as what I would do without a coat, as so many people had to do. Mother said that I need to keep better care of my things.

A friend had told me that in difficult situations, to write Mother a letter as to what I had done and why. I left it on the counter in the kitchen, so she would see it. I had been taught that by writing a letter, she would have time to cool down before I got back from school. That worked wonders.

So on the third day, the truth was finally out. I had lent the coat to a friend without a coat. As I had several coats, I did not see the harm in giving one away. Since she had gotten the letter, she did not go ballistic. But she was glad that I had been so giving. My fear of her reaction is what made me lie in the first place.

Understanding and respect of the situation put a whole new light on it. Honesty is the always best policy, even if it hurts. When she calmed down, Mother had to admit that I have several coats. So there was not a need to rush out to replace the coat.

Things to remember:

* Write a letter.
* Figure out how to help the situation.
* Writing it down
* Tell it to someone you trust.
* Where can you find them?
* Will telling some one help?
* Stay in the present.

Writing a letter can soften the sting of a parents' reaction. So the parents will have time to think about it before they go into a rage. I know that God is in charge. He will help me if I ask. I was grateful to the friend who had told me to write the letter to Mother. This helped me to get understanding and respect from her for being generous with my old coat.

My Coat

CHAPTER 11
FINDING MY WAY

Sometimes it's easy to get confused in a strange neighborhood or even a familiar one. It can be easy to panic, but remember, all roads lead somewhere and these days, you can usually ask someone for help or consult a map.

Am I lost? Do I know where I need to go? Do I know where I am now? Which way do I need to go? What street do I need to be on? Am I moving in the correct direction? Or have I lost my way?

Am I on the correct road? Are there signs that say the street names and the side street's name? What can I expect to see? Are there signs that will help?

There may be more than one way to get where I need to go. That can be confusing. Look for familiar signs. But remember, there are lots of the same stores, like big box stores. That can be confusing. That has really confused me before.

Do I have a map? There should be one in every car. That will help if I get lost. There is a device call a GPS which can be programmed to help locate the place that you are going.

Can I ask someone for help? Is there someone I can ask for directions? Who can get me to a place I know? Is there someone who can draw a map? Or write down directions to help me?

What is the name of the street that I need next? Are there unusual signs in the area - like an unusual billboard, that will help guide me? What is my next move? Am I ignoring the signs that I need? Am I paying attention to what I am seeing?

Points to remember:

* Bring the phone number with you as to where you are going.
* Keep a detailed map in your car at all times
* Go to mapquest.com for directions
* Use a GPS to help find your way.
* Get directions from the place that you are going

With all the ways to find your directions, I wish you a good trip and a peaceful one. Enjoy the scenery and look for new things. Look forward to getting where you are going, and prepare for you trip, ask God to go with you and smooth the way as you go.

Traffic Intersection

CHAPTER

12

EMERGENCIES

Find someone who can solve your problem. Do not be afraid to ask for help. Other people may know what you need. Accidents happen. That is part of being human. In these modern times, almost every one has a cell phone. Way back we were told to keep a quarter with us in case of emergencies. Back then there were pay phones around. The pay phones have mostly disappeared, because of cell phones. Modern devices can help keep me safe. A cell phone is very important to keep us safe.

In fact, my cell phone literally saved my life. I broke my nose. At that time, I was the only one in a big building because I had gotten to the meeting early. I wanted to prepare the room for the meeting. This included making the room smaller by moving the collapsible wall. The collapsible wall gave faster than I anticipated. I lunged forward and lost my balance. I broke my nose on the stationary wall. I am grateful that I had my cell with me and so I called 9-1-1. The dispatcher was able to get me the help that I needed. The only information that I could give them was the name of the church and the road that it was on. When the ambulance arrived, they called out and I was able to call out where I was. I was grateful that the ambulance found me, and took me to the nearest hospital.

I was able to get someone to pick me up at the hospital, and drive me to my car. Thank goodness I could drive because I was a long way from home.

Points to remember:

* Stay in the present.
* Look for your choices.
* Who do you trust?
* Where can you find them?
* Are they a cell phone call away?
* Will telling someone help?

You need more than one choice. The first choice may not really be the best! Turn it over to God! I was grateful that I knew someone who could help get my nose fixed. My ear, nose and throat doctor needed to straighten my nose. Friends said I looked like a Star Wars character with the splint that had to be on my nose! Now I have a straight nose!

CHAPTER

13

TRIPS

Before going on a trip, I make a spreadsheet with the details of the trip. I include a budget and all the facts as they become available. Check the Internet for directions and find a map of the area. Do you have a computer that you can use? My understanding is that a GPS is a computer which is portable for use in cars and boats.

If you do not have access to a computer, there are libraries in most cities. Most libraries have computers with Internet connections that you can use. Computers and modern ideas can make our lives easier, if we let them.

For example, these sites have been helpful to me: www.google.com has good maps. Put in the town that you are going to and you can get an entire map of the town. You can enlarge and move all over the town. Www.Mapquest.com also gives directions.

With a spreadsheet containing all the information as to my flights numbers, hotels, and phone numbers to call, and cost estimates of all that I am going to do. The addresses are necessary for the GPS. Many cell phones let you have access to the internet.

This helps me to be sure that I have all I need for the trip. With the spreadsheet on the front of the binder, I am always sure what I need to do next. That way I can enjoy my trip more and eliminate the surprises of not being organized or not having enough money.

I have found in my travels that making a binder of the information I will need is a big help in keeping me connected to where I am and where I need to go. In the binder, I take the computer directions from Mapquest, and have the map of the place. I did follow on a map of the area the direction that I was given on Mapquest. This has been a big help in being sure where I needed to go.

When I went to my niece's wedding in Pennsylvania, I did that and so I had no fear of being lost. I felt comfortable driving to where I needed to go, as I had memorized the map of the towns that I was going to. My brother gave me the name of the motel and where it was located.

The first night was spent by the airport. That way I can see the traffic on the TV before I get on my way for my adventure. Before leaving the motel, review the maps and get your binder organized for what you will see that day. Staying at a motel has worked best for me, because I am usually tired from flying. Most motels, by the airports, have a shuttle to and from the airport. That works for me. Then I can get the rental car the next day and saved a day's rent on the car and not need to worry about finding the motel.

Points to remember:

* Planned your trip
* What do you want to see?
* Stay in the present.
* Look for your choices.
* Write down your choices.

* Write down who and what to see.
* Where can you find them?
* Will telling someone help?

With my trip spreadsheet, I am able to better enjoy my trip and the people who I am going to see and my whole adventure. On my spreadsheet the choices are put for me to make. The first choice may not really be the best! Turn it over to God! He will help you enjoy your trip and help you to stay organized to help support peace of mind. In the front of the binder goes the paper for the day. I can see the maps that I will be using at the current moment. The binder is substantial enough that I am not dealing with flimsy papers and I can concentrate on my sightseeing.

		Trip to neice's wedding		
		dates -		
Airfare		Southwest Airlines		900
		flight # 123		
		Conf # 9876543		
	date	leave Austin	11:00 AM	
		Arrive Baltimore	3:30 PM	
	date	Leave Baltimore	11:30 AM	
		flight # 345		
		Arrive Austin	3:30 PM	
Rental Car		rent at airport		60
		Enterprise		
		dates		
		Conf # 6789043		
Motel		Days Inn		150
		Address		
		days		
		Conf #		
Food				200
Gas for car				100
Parking at Austin airport				50
Sightseeing and souvenirs				65
			TOTAL	1545

Budget of Trip to Niece's Wedding

CHAPTER

14

LOSING THINGS

Small things can give us panic attacks also, like losing keys. I lost my keys. Where could they be? It helps if things have a home, a place where they are automatically put when we set them down. My keys go on the counter by the door. That is where I keep a spare car key and a spare door key. I keep a spare car key in my purse and a spare door key in my car. You can figure out what will work best for you.

Points to remember:

* The keys are somewhere.
* Small things need a home,
* A place where they are safe.
* Look for your choices.
* Write your choices down.
* Who do you trust?

When you are stuck and cannot go where you need to go, it may feel like a major thing. There may be help if you write and ask God for help and look for your choices. Do I have a spare set of keys? Is there the one that I need on them? Where are they? Could they be in this room? Are they in plain sight? Are they in something? Could they be in my purse? Are they in my home? Did I leave them in the car? Where could they be? Where did I see them last?

On my way home from Colorado, the place where my dog was staying was not open when I got there, so I took a nap and took some pictures. Then my dog ran to me as they opened. When we got settled in the car, I could not find the car keys. There was a spare key in the car. That is how we got home. Then when we arrived home, I had left a key with a neighbor to water my plants and look after things. So we had a way to get into home.

I needed to turn it over to my Higher Power. How important is it? It was important to get home in the car. Do I really need it? Yes, I really needed the car keys. What will happen if I do not find it? That set of keys never showed up, but I was ok because of the spare keys. I have found that it is a good idea to keep more that one set of keys for when I can not find them.

If it is meant to be mine, I will find them in God's time. My time is not necessarily God's time. Well, I can't find it? Do I have to have them? What am I going to do? Do I need it now? Is it necessary?

There are places that can replace keys. Locksmiths and sometimes the auto dealership can help. One time I locked my keys in the car, and a locksmith can get them out easily. Last time that happened, a friend told me that cab companies may carry equipment with them to open car doors. That took a lot less time than the locksmith.

It is frustrating to lose your keys or anything else. We need to remember that we are human and that this is part of being human. God will help us if we can calm down and do the next right thing.

Picture of Keys

CHAPTER

15

ORGANIZATION

There are many ways to get organized. You need to decide which will work best for you. Here are a few of the ways. What works best for me is to have a book with the sheets that I have enclosed to list the various activities. A computer has various programs to help with the task. There is also the bulletin board. I also have a calendar on my fridge to plan my month and year. Other people have a small calendar in their purse.

What do you need to get done now? That is important for you to remember? I have really gotten stressed with lots of things to get done. As I write down the things that need to get done, that takes them from my mind and I can concentrate on what I am doing, thus getting it done better and with less stress. Stress is one thing that causes panic attacks. Remember to write down things. So you can stay on top of the important things. Many people in business have what is called a Daytimer.

On my fridge at home, there is a calendar on which I put the things to do of the day. Some things have a scheduled time, like doctor's appointments. Before I make needed plans I need to consult my calendar. My life can not function with out checking my calendar. When a new activity comes, I have to say I need to check my calendar. May I call you and confirm.

When activities are scheduled in advance, I like to check the day of the activity, to make sure the activity is still ok with the other person. That has saved me many an anxious moment.

As I calm down from the stresses of every day life, with my list, this makes the day go more smoothly, and more peaceful. It is always rewarding to be able to check off things on the list. As some things get taken off of the list, more things may surface, things that are more important and need to be put to the top of the list.

Also, it is good to number the things to be done and do them in order of most important and also there may be things to do where time needs to be considered. The time needs to be includes on the Daytimer.

The day needs to be scheduled by calls to be made, times that need to be considered and things to be done. This will help to organize your day to get the most benefit out of your time.

On the list of calls always include the phone number so the calls can be made when you are sitting and waiting for a scheduled activity to begin if there is some quite. Thanks to cell phones. The errands can be scheduled on the way to your events or your way home from events. Just recently I went to an event and got there really early, so I left and went and did an errand. That felt good to get the nearby errand crossed off of my list and to have all of my calls caught up to date. With the price of gas, it helps to be organized as to the order of things to do.

It helps to keep a grocery list on the fridge, so every time you realize you are out of something, or want something, you can write it down immediately, instead of forgetting about it. When grocery time comes, I check the fridge, pantry, and the bathroom for other things that may be needed.

Points to remember:

* Stay in the present.
* Look for your choices.
* Write them down.
* Who do you need to call?
* Where are the things you need to do?
* Where can you find them?
* Will telling someone help?

Here is to a peaceful, productive day with all that is needed to be accomplished being accomplished in God's time and way. That was a good day, hope yours was also. If things did not all get done, there is always tomorrow. Since the things have been numbered in importance, I am peaceful, and hope you are also. Some days there is too much to do and only so many hours in the day.

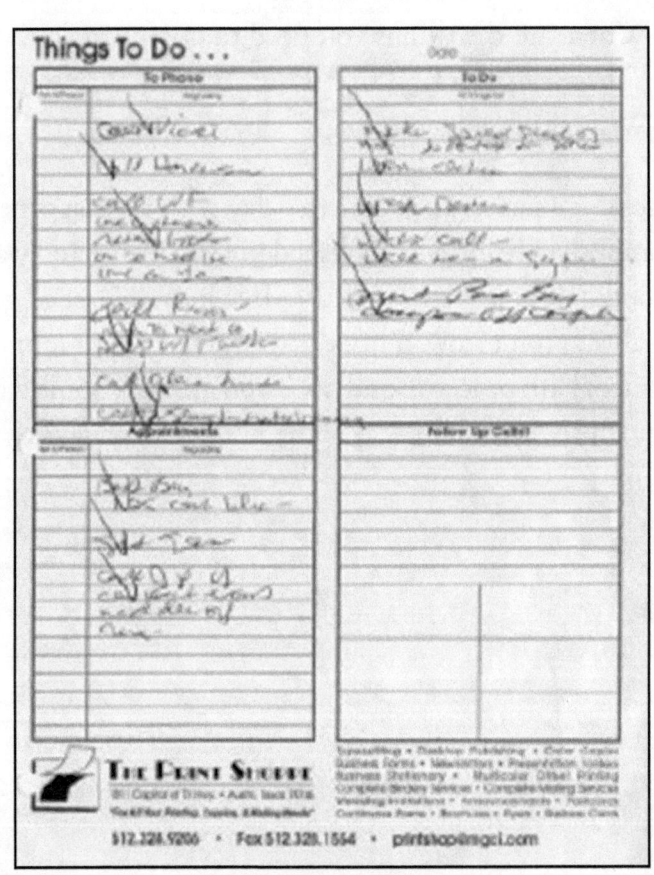

Daytimer Page

CHAPTER

16

LOSING A PET

Many of us have a pet. The care of them is necessary and rewarding. Dogs need to be walked and cats use a litter box. As I was walking my dog, she ran away. Has this ever happened to you? Our feelings can be really hurt and we get scared about their safety.

When I was out walking my dog, I let her off her leash. I knew better than to do that, but I did it anyway. She got away from me. I sat down and cried. How will I find her? Do I have a picture of her? Where does she like to go? I looked in all the places that I would think. What does she like to do? Where did I last see her? Where has she been going lately? Which way did she go? I followed where I saw her go. Who can I ask for help?

It can help to put up signs with her picture on it and my phone number and offer a reward. Most lost dogs, especially without tags, find their way to an animal shelter. It is important for your pet to have a collar, with your phone number on it, so you can be called to claim her. That makes everyone happy!

Finally I was able to make my way home. She was in our apartment before me. She had been taken to the manager's office. They put her in our apartment. She had her ID tags with our address and phone number on, so the lady who found her knew where to take her, so I would get her back. That was a happy ending to a sad situation. I was grateful to have her back.

Points to remember:

* Stay in the present.
* Was she protected with a collar?
* Look for your choices.
* Write down your choices.
* Who do you trust?
* Where can you find them?
* Will telling someone help?

Another way to lose a pet is for her to get attacked while we were out walking. We had been minding our own business, having a good walk, when a large dog came racing toward us. He took a big hunk out of my dog's neck. I was able to pull the big dog off of my little 10 pound poodle mix. Then he turned on me, as I saw that I turned loose of him, and yelled for the owner to come get his dog.

My dog did not want me to pick her up. I was very grateful when a car stopped to help us. They had a cell. They were able to find a pet emergency clinic. I did not have my purse with me, so they took me to our home and went and got my purse. It really hurt that my dog did not what me to hold her. This couple was able to find the emergency clinic. They were happy to take us there. We had to leave her, so the couple took me home. She was ready to come home in a couple of hours.

Points to remember:

* God is in charge.
* All will turn out as it needs to.
* Stay in the moment.
* What are your choices?
* Stay in the moment.

A third way to lose a pet is by her getting sick. Some times she will recover and sometimes she will not. Over the life of a pet, it is important for her to go with a vet as needed. Pets can get cancer the same as humans. My dog Bonne's cancer was caught early so all that she had to have was surgery.

The thing that killed her was that she got kidney disease. The treatment was to put fluids in her. There was no way that I could have done this by myself. I shared this in a meeting. A handsome guy approached me after the meeting and offered to help. He was a life saver. He came over and helped put the fluids in my cute little dog. That worked for about 6 weeks. Then it got harder to do, and my baby was getting tired of the highs and lows. So we stopped the fluids. The vet said that she would let me know when she was ready to go to sleep. We went for another 6 weeks. On a Friday afternoon, she threw up, which was the sign the vet told me to watch for. A friend had offered to be there for me, so I called her to come, and she did. There was no way that I could have done that on my own.

When she was going to be put to sleep, I told her she was going to see my dad and her boyfriend. So she went with a smile on her face.

Pet's lives are not as long as human's lives. My dog had been with me for 12 years. She is still missed. Friends told me to get another pet. I was not ready, but about 6 weeks later I found a cute little cat. Our picture is on the back of the book. As I have had surgeries, it has been easier to care for my cat, rather than having a dog to walk. My cat requires to be walked, so I am still able to be outside with her. Have you ever seen a cat on a leash? Where we live all pets are required to be on a leash. That includes cats. I am happy with how we do with this law.

Hope this helps bring you comfort and a vision for help!

I wish for you peace, happiness, health, safety and serenity!

Bonne

POEMS

Claustrophobic

What should I do?
What can I do?
What do I feel like doing?
What are my choices?
Can I walk?
Can I fly?
Can I swim?
Can I play?
What do I need to do?
What are my needs?
Can I do them by myself?
Do I need help?
Who can do what I need help with?
What are my choices?
I have choices.
God has been generous with getting my needs met.
I am really claustrophobic with all my choices!
I have so many choices I do not know what to do.
What do I want to do?
What really needs to be done?
Do I like myself?
Am I comfortable with myself?
What do I need to do to be serene?

Found

Overwhelmed
By the things to learn
By my teachers
By the beauty of nature
As I see in my dreams
That I have choices
To travel and to see
I long to be free
To travel and to see
That I have choices
As I see in my dreams.
By the beauty of nature
By my teachers
By the things to learn
Overwhelmed

STRESS

What is stress?
How am I affected?
When do I feel stress?
Help me to realize when this happens.
My body aches
My head races
My mind gets confused
My body will not rest
What can I do when I feel stressed?
Tried resting
Tried reading
Tried exercising
What I need to do is to relax
Let my mind rest
Let my body just be
Not expect too much of myself.

Plan For Me

God has a plan for me.
I have no idea where He is leading.
I have faith that it is for my good.
I have been experiencing the miracles.
When I feel overwhelmed,
He says peddle,
Put one foot in front of the other.
He helps me do that.
When I need money, it comes.
When I need quiet time, it comes.
When I need love, it comes.
When I need to be creative, it comes.
I know that God loves me.
I do the best that I can.
That is all that God asks.
I am grateful for where God is leading me.

Dreams

Where do I want to go?
What do I want to see?
There is the beauty of the USA?
Looking forward to being a gypsy,
Following the wind and the weather,
Cutting my own path.
Being on the road in my Class A RV
Enjoying nature – seeing the wild animals
Seeing the wonderful natural beauty.
Following the weather
During the winter, in the south
During the summer, in the north.
Going slow as to not miss anything
Going slow as to find my sanctuary
Going slow to find my peace.
I want to see it all.
I want to take pictures of it all.
The beauty that is the USA.

Expectations Met

Thank you for my health.
Thank you for leading me to my education.
Thank you for my mentors.
Thank you for your guidance.
Know that all will be well.
That all is on track.
That I will get my RV.
That I will be a famous photographer and writer.
Maybe even have my person sought after.
Sure not interested in that
Want to make a good living on my own.
Will I be prosperous and have all that I want and need.
The pyridine is shifting.
The healing is coming.
The help is coming for peace.
Serenity is coming.
Have come a long way in releasing
Hurt people - Hurt people
Mom is a hurt person.
God grant us peace and serenity.
She has always been the perfect actress.
God knows all of her problems,
Mental as well as physical.
Know what she will allow me to know.

Thank you for my teachers,
Thank you for my growth,
Thank you for my opening.
Thank you for my gratitude.
Thank you for calling my overwhelming,
Thank you for opening the doors,

Thank you for my discoveries,
Thank you for helping the words to flow.

God Poem

God
Lead Me
Guide Me
Strengthen Me
Show me the way
To peace and serenity.
You lead
And I will follow.
I trust that
You know the way.
To peace and serenity
I am Yours.

www.ingramcontent.com/pod-product-compliance
Lightning Source LLC
LaVergne TN
LVHW041540060526
838200LV00037B/1067